MINUTE MYSTERIES

BRAINTEASERS, PUZZLERS, AND STORIES TO SOLVE

★ American Girl™

Published by Pleasant Company Publications
Copyright © 2006 by American Girl, LLC
All rights reserved. No part of this book may be used or reproduced in
any manner whatsoever without written permission except in the case of
brief quotations embodied in critical articles and reviews.

Questions or comments? Call 1-800-845-0005,
visit our Web site at **americangirl.com**, or write to Customer Service,
American Girl, 8400 Fairway Place, Middleton, WI 53562.

Printed in China
06 07 08 09 10 LEO 12 11 10 9 8 7 6 5 4 3 2 1

American Girl™ and its associated logos, Molly®, Kit®, Samantha™,
Addy®, Josefina®, Felicity®, and Kaya® are trademarks of
American Girl, LLC.

Written by Jennifer Hirsch and Teri Witkowski
Designed by Justin King
Produced by Jeannette Bailey, Julie Kimmell, Judith Lary,
and Richmond Powers
Illustrations by Dan Andreasen, Nick Backes, Bill Farnsworth,
Renée Graef, Susan McAliley, Walter Rane, Dahl Taylor,
and Jean-Paul Tibbles

Cataloging-in-Publication Data
available from the Library of Congress.

TABLE OF CONTENTS

 Kit poked her head out the train window and waved good-bye to Ruthie, Stirling, and her parents. Then, as the train started to move, she sat down beside Aunt Millie. At last, they were off on their journey to visit Charlie, her brother, in Montana. Kit knew she would miss everyone at home, but

4

she was excited to think of all the interesting new people she would meet on her trip.

"You're as jumpy as a jackrabbit," Aunt Millie told her. "You go on now and explore the train while I take a little catnap."

Happily, Kit jumped up and headed for the observation car. It had huge windows on both sides, with the seats facing the aisle. Kit was pleased to see three girls about her age crowded on one of the seats, staring out the window opposite. It would be fun to have new friends on the train trip! Were they sisters? Kit wondered. They didn't look much alike.

Kit sat down across from the three girls and gave them a friendly smile. "Hi, I'm Kit," she said. "What's your name?"

A girl with curly brown hair smiled back. "I'm Joanie, and this is Frankie," she said, gesturing to the redhead beside her.

"Are you sisters?" Kit asked. She had always thought it would be nice to have a sister.

"No, just pals," said Joanie. "We all met on the train."

"I'm Georgia," said the third girl, who had short blond hair like Kit's. "Pleased to meet you, Kit. What's your last name?"

"Kittredge," Kit replied. "It's easy to remember if you just think of my first name, because the two names sort of match—Kit Kittredge." She smiled again. "What are your last names?"

Georgia, Joanie, and Frankie looked at each other and started laughing.

"I don't get it—what's the joke?" Kit asked.

"You'll get it when you hear our last names," said Frankie, still giggling.

"Let me tell her," Joanie sputtered, trying to keep a straight face. "Our last names are Frank, Jones, and St. George."

"But none of our first and last names match, the way yours do," Frankie chimed in.

Kit paused and thought this over. "So your name isn't . . ."

"Frankie Frank!" said Frankie, and again the girls burst into gales of laughter, with Kit joining them this time. "No, my parents didn't name me that, thank goodness! My name is Frankie Jones."

"Can you figure out what Joanie's and my last names are?" Georgia asked Kit.

Kit thought for a minute, then nodded.

What were the names of Kit's new friends? The answers are on page 60.

"Hurry up, Kirsten!" Lisbeth called. "We're going to be late for the first day of school."

Kirsten walked carefully up the path from the stream. It had rained the night before, and the way was muddy. Kirsten had also filled the water bucket too full, and now the water sloshed over the edge and onto her shoe. But the puddles and her care not to spill more water weren't the only things slowing Kirsten's steps. She felt dizzy, the way she'd felt on the ship just before she was seasick. Her stomach fluttered as though a bird were inside her. The thought of going to a school where no one knew her and everyone spoke a different language was making Kirsten very nervous.

"Here's your lunch *tine*," Lisbeth said after Kirsten set the bucket of water in the house. She slipped her arm through Kirsten's. "Don't worry," she reassured her cousin. "I know it's hard to be the new girl, but

tine

you'll do fine. Just do what I do."

Kirsten tried to be calm, but when they reached Powderkeg School, the fluttering in her stomach grew worse. She felt very small as she followed Lisbeth into the large room. Her brothers, Lars and Peter, were the only other people who looked familiar.

Lisbeth led Kirsten to the benches on the girls' side of the room. As they sat down, Lisbeth whispered, "We have a new teacher."

A young woman in a black dress tapped the stove with a ruler to get everyone's attention. "I am Miss Winston," she said in a crisp voice. "I've come west from Camden, Maine. I'm to be your teacher."

"You don't look any older than me," a black-haired boy said out loud. He did not hide the surprise in his voice.

"That's Amos Anderson!" Lisbeth whispered.

Miss Winston faced Amos. "You will not talk out of turn in my classroom," she said sternly.

Kirsten's face grew hot. Would Lisbeth get

9

into trouble for whispering? Kirsten saw Amos
grin and look down at his big hands. He had
broad shoulders and the beginnings of a black
mustache. Kirsten thought he looked more like
a man than a boy.

"Now you know my name," Miss Winston
continued. "But I don't know yours. I'd like
each of you to come forward and introduce
yourselves to me politely. We are ladies and
gentlemen here at Powderkeg School."

One by one the girls got up and introduced
themselves. Kirsten dreaded walking out
there in the middle of the room with everyone
watching her. She was the last girl to take her
turn. The floor seemed to move under her as
she stepped forward. "Kirsten Larson," she
muttered.

Before she could escape back to the bench,
Miss Winston said firmly, "Say 'Kirsten Larson,
ma'am.'"

"Ma'am," Kirsten repeated. But the word
didn't sound right. She felt a blush prickle
at the base of her throat. Then Kirsten heard

Amos laughing at her halting English.

Miss Winston's eyes narrowed. Then she raised her ruler over her head and brought it smashing down on the top of the iron stove. The crack went through the room like the shot of a rifle.

"You will not laugh at one another's efforts," she announced. Miss Winston motioned for Kirsten to sit down. Then she looked at Amos. "I would like you to introduce yourself next," she said.

Amos stood up. He was much taller than Miss Winston. "Amos Anderson, ma'am," he said.

"Which reading book are you using, Amos?" Miss Winston asked him.

"I finished the third one, ma'am." He winked at the girls' bench.

"Only the third? How old are you?" Miss Winston asked.

"I'm nineteen," Amos drawled. "Same as you."

Miss Winston tapped her palm with her

ruler and considered him. "Yes, Amos, I am nineteen too. But I am the teacher and you are the student. I'm here to help you read and do sums the way a man must if he wants to make his way in the world. Please set a good example for the others."

Amos's face turned red. He had seemed so bold before. Now it looked as though the fluttering that had been in Kirsten's stomach was in his. "Why don't I go draw a bucket of water so that the children can all have a drink before we start in reading," he said.

"Thank you, Amos. That's a good idea," Miss Winston agreed. Amos grabbed one of the wooden water buckets and walked quickly out of the schoolhouse.

While Kirsten and the others waited for their drink of water, Miss Winston led the class in a song. Amos was not back when they finished, so Miss Winston began passing out the books, small slates, and slate pencils. She looked at her timepiece as students began copying the alphabet onto their slates. Kirsten had copied all the way up to J, and Amos *still* hadn't returned. Kirsten was beginning to wonder if he had decided not to come back at all when Amos finally stomped up the schoolhouse steps. Everyone turned to look as he set the bucket, filled to the top with water, on the bench.

"Girls first," Amos said, calmly picking up the dipper as if no time had passed at all.

Before anyone could move, Miss Winston said, "Amos Anderson, that was an excessively long time to be gone fetching water." She looked around the room. "You will not dawdle with any of your work while you are in my classroom," she warned everyone.

"It was too muddy to cut across the field," Amos explained. "I had to take the long way around on the path. But I ran all the way back. Ma'am."

Miss Winston looked at Amos closely. "Very well," she sighed. "Girls first."

There were murmurs as the girls lined up

for their drinks. Kirsten stood behind Lisbeth, and she leaned close so no one else could hear her. "Amos is telling a falsehood," Kirsten said. "He didn't run all the way back."

Lisbeth looked at her cousin in surprise. "Amos is bold, but I don't think he would lie. What makes you think so?"

Why did Kirsten think Amos had lied? Check your answer on page 59.

"Riddle me this, Addy," said Sam. "Where's the only place it makes sense to put a cart before a horse?"

Addy loved trying to guess her brother's riddles. It was a game they played often. "I know it's not a stable. How about an unstable?" Addy asked.

Sam laughed. "That's pretty clever," he said. "But the place where cart goes before horse is the dictionary."

"That's a good one, Sam," Addy said.

Addy held her brother's hand, doing her best to keep up with his long stride. It was a dreary Sunday with clouds low in the sky, but Addy was happy. Sam was walking her to her friend Sarah's.

"I've got another one for you," Sam said as they turned onto Seventh Street. "How is a piano like a door?"

"Hmmm," Addy answered. She was quiet for a few minutes as she thought about the riddle. Sam whistled softly as though he had

stumped Addy for good. But then she smiled. "I think I know the answer. But first, you riddle me this: What has teeth but doesn't bite?"

Can you solve Sam's and Addy's riddles? The answers are on page 59.

"The corn harvest has been good this year," said Josefina as she peeled back the husk from an ear of roasted corn. She and her sisters were going to braid the husks together to make a long string of ears so that the corn could be hung up to dry in the hot New Mexico sun. Once the corn was dry, it would keep all winter. Carmen, the cook, would use the dried corn kernels in soup and stew, or grind them into flour to make tortillas.

Francisca eyed the large bowl of roasted ears and sighed. "This will take forever," she complained.

"Many hands make light work, Francisca," Ana, the eldest, reminded her.

Francisca, who was fifteen and the second-eldest, rolled her eyes. "You sound just like Tía Dolores."

"*Gracias*," replied Ana with a smile. "You have paid me a great compliment."

Francisca huffed in annoyance. "Tía Dolores always goes around with those little sayings,

18

Treasure in the Corn

just to make us work harder."

"Was there something else you wanted to be doing right now, Francisca?" asked Clara, who was twelve. "Working on your sewing, perhaps?"

Josefina smiled to herself. Clara knew that Francisca liked sewing even less than husking corn.

"All right, girls," Ana chided gently. "Let's not bicker."

"Tell us a story, Ana," said Josefina. "That will help to pass the time."

Ana nodded and picked up another ear of corn. "I remember one year long ago when the corn harvest was not as good as this one, and the corn was full of ear worms," she began. "But it was all we had, so we still had to roast and dry the ears. The roasting killed the worms, and when we peeled the husks back, the dead worms would fall out." Ana glanced with amusement at her sisters, who were listening with their noses wrinkled in disgust.

"But one of you found a worm that was still

alive," Ana continued. "You were so excited to discover a tiny green worm still wriggling in the corncob that you began jumping up and down, shouting, 'I found a treasure! I found a treasure! Lucky, lucky me!'"

Josefina, Clara, and Francisca stared at one another in disbelief.

"A worm?" Francisca snorted. "How revolting! Whoever thought a *worm* was a treasure?"

"Well, I'm sure *I* would never say a silly thing like that," said practical Clara.

What a funny story! thought Josefina. Could it have been about her, when she was very small? "Which one of us was it, Ana?" asked Josefina, her eyes shining with excitement.

"Yes, tell us! Tell us who it was!" demanded Francisca and Clara.

Ana smiled mischievously. "When this story happened, I was as old as Clara is now. The one who found the worm was one-third of Francisca's age now. Josefina, you were one-sixth as old as I was and one-fourth as old as Francisca was."

Francisca, Clara, and Josefina narrowed their eyes and began figuring numbers in their heads. Their hands continued peeling and braiding cornhusks, but they were concentrating so hard, they didn't even notice when they reached the end of the pile. Suddenly Francisca looked up. "Oh my—we've finished the corn!"

"Yes, but you haven't solved the story of the worm, and you can't leave until you do!" Ana teased.

Josefina jumped up. "I've got it! I know who it was!" she shouted, waving her last ear of corn in the air.

Who found the worm? And how old were the four sisters at the time? *Turn to page 59 for the answers.*

Samantha and her friends gasped with delight as Mrs. Hawkins carried out the tray of ten tiny cakes all glowing with candles. Everyone sang "Happy Birthday," and then Samantha leaned forward and blew out all the candles in one whoosh as the other girls clapped.

"This is such an elegant party," said Agnes as Mrs. Hawkins served her a petit four.

"Would you care for some ice cream?" asked Samantha in her most grown-up voice. She passed Agnes a small dish with ice cream that was shaped like a scalloped shell.

"Oh! Molded ice cream!" chirped Ruth. "Just like in a fancy ice cream parlor!"

"And wait till you taste it!" exclaimed Agatha.

All the girls put rather large, unladylike spoonfuls into their mouths. Their faces turned as pink as the ice cream.

"Ugh!"

"Eew!"

"Ick!"

The girls coughed and choked. They spat the ice cream out into their napkins. They slurped down gulps of lemonade. They sputtered and gasped and gagged.

"Salt!" Samantha gasped. "This ice cream is full of salt!"

"That rotten Eddie Ryland!" said Agnes. "I bet he put the salt in our ice cream!"

The Ice Cream Culprit

"Where is he? I'll fix him," Agatha threatened.

"Let's go find him!" said Ida.

Still pink-faced with indignation, the girls got up from the table and marched into the side yard where Hawkins, the Butler, had set up the ice cream freezer. Eddie was nowhere to be seen. Then Samantha spotted him on the other side of the lilac hedge that ran between Grandmary's yard and the Rylands'.

"Eddie Ryland, shame on you!" called Samantha, as the girls approached him.

"For what?" said Eddie without looking up. He was squinting at a croquet ball. Suddenly he swung the wooden mallet down and—*plock!*—the painted ball shot through the hoop. Eddie looked up with an expression of triumph.

"For ruining Samantha's elegant birthday party," said Ruth.

"Well, the whole party wasn't ruined, Ruth. Just the ice cream," said Ida.

"That was supposed to be the best part!" said Samantha. All the effort Hawkins had gone to, pressing each serving of ice cream into a little shaped mold, just to make it special for her birthday! "Instead, it was the worst part."

"And all because of you, Eddie," Agatha added.

"Me? I didn't put any salt in your ice cream. I've been over here playing with my new croquet set," Eddie said. "And I'm pretty good at it, too. Watch!" He turned his back on her and walked to the croquet ball, lining up his mallet for the next swing.

Agnes glared at him. "We still think you did it, Eddie!"

"You can think what you want, but you can't prove it," Eddie retorted.

Samantha narrowed her eyes. "Oh yes, we can!"

How could Samantha prove that Eddie was the culprit? *Turn to page 60 to find out.*

Up in Kit's attic bedroom, Kit and her friends Ruthie and Stirling were creating a new issue of their newspaper, *The Hard Times News.* Kit was bent over her typewriter in silent concentration. Well, not exactly silent. The clackety-clacking of the keys made a constant din as Kit typed her story.

Finally, she was finished. With satisfaction, Kit rolled the paper out of her typewriter and handed it to Stirling. "I left some space for you to add an illustration," she told him. Then she rolled a fresh sheet of blank white paper into her typewriter and stared at it with a little flutter of anticipation. What to write about next?

Kit thought and thought, but nothing came to her. She had already reported on her visit to the soup kitchen, and how many eggs Aunt Millie's chickens were laying each day, and the latest mishap of Grace, the basset hound. Nothing else newsworthy was going on.

"Ruthie, how much space do you think your story will take up?" Kit asked. Maybe Ruthie's would fill up the whole second page, and Kit wouldn't need another story.

Ruthie held up her sheet of paper. It was about half full. "Here's where I'm at so far, and I'm almost finished. When I'm done, shall I cut it out so we can glue it onto your page?"

Kit thought for a moment. "No, that would be too messy," she said, pulling the clean sheet out of her typewriter. "I'll just add something

to the bottom of your page when you're finished."

But when Ruthie handed her the page, Kit still hadn't come up with any ideas. She rolled the sheet with Ruthie's story into her typewriter. There really wasn't a lot of space left on the page. She just needed one little item to fill the space—maybe just a puzzle or riddle, to entertain her readers. Kit stared down at her typewriter, waiting for inspiration to strike.

Suddenly an idea came to Kit, and she began to type:

```
Riddle

Here is a sequence of letters:

     Z  X  C  V  B  N

What letter comes next?
```

Can you solve Kit's riddle?
The answer is on page 59.

An Amusing Drive

"Climb in, girls!" said Uncle Gard. Samantha and Nellie helped Bridget and Jenny step up onto the running board of the long black automobile. Giggling with excitement, the little girls slid onto the front seat.

"Ooh, it's leather!" exclaimed Bridget, running her hand along the seat.

"It's bouncy!" said Jenny, bouncing up and down.

"Settle down, Jenny," Nellie scolded gently. "You wouldn't bounce on the parlor sofa, would you?"

Samantha's uncle smiled. "Don't worry, Nellie. This is a motorcar, not a sofa. It won't break from a little bouncing. In fact, the seat's made to bounce, so that if I hit a rock while I'm driving, I won't break—I'll bounce!"

Jenny and Bridget giggled and repeated to each other, "He won't break—he'll bounce!" with great delight.

Samantha flushed with pride and affection. Uncle Gard was so kind and funny!

An Amusing Drive

"All right, girls, hang on to your hats while I crank this engine to life." At the front of the automobile, Uncle Gard turned a large handle vigorously. The motorcar gave a sputter and then a smooth rumble. Samantha and Nellie climbed into the backseat and Uncle Gard slid behind the wheel, and they were off.

When their drive was over, Samantha was famished. "I hope Gertrude has a big lunch for us," she said, stepping onto the curb.

"Me too," Bridget and Jenny agreed as they

clambered out of the car.

"I'm so hungry, I could eat a horse," said Uncle Gard. "Or a house," he added, setting off another gale of giggles.

"Come along now, girls," Nellie said to her sisters. She and Samantha led them inside through the front door, while Uncle Gard parked the automobile.

As Aunt Cornelia helped the little girls wash up for lunch, Bridget and Jenny told her every detail of their wonderful ride in the motorcar, complete with Uncle Gard's jokes. Aunt Cornelia nodded as she listened, smiling at their giddy enthusiasm, but suddenly she frowned and looked troubled.

Uncle Gard came in the back door and joined them at the dining table. "We've had a most memorable morning motoring," he reported grandly to Aunt Cornelia, as they all sat down to eat.

Aunt Cornelia nodded. "So I'm told," she said, and Samantha saw the troubled look flash across her face again. "In fact," Cornelia

An Amusing Drive

went on, "I hear that you have perhaps become slightly reckless in your driving habits."

Uncle Gard stopped with a spoonful of soup halfway to his mouth. "Reckless? With this precious cargo aboard?" Slowly he lowered his spoon back into the soup bowl. "My dear, whatever can you mean?"

Cornelia put her hand on his and spoke gently. "Gardner, I know you simply meant to give the girls a thrill, but it's very important to stop the motorcar when you hit an obstacle, and not simply continue on as if nothing had happened."

Samantha looked at Nellie in surprise. What was her aunt talking about? They hadn't hit anything during their drive! Nellie shrugged and shook her head, looking as puzzled as Samantha felt.

Suddenly Bridget burst out laughing. "Miss Cornelia, I think you misunderstood!"

What had Cornelia misunderstood? Turn to page 59 to find out.

Giggles in the Garden

Felicity hurried up the steps of Miss Manderly's house clutching a small bunch of flowers. *Am I late?* she worried as she rushed inside. Felicity had stopped in her garden to pick a few spring blossoms for her teacher. The air was fresh and the sun was warm, and soon Felicity had lost all track of time. She had run all the way to Miss Manderly's, and now she was relieved to see that lessons had not yet begun. Felicity tucked a loose strand of hair behind her ear, hid the flowers behind her back, and joined Elizabeth and Annabelle in the parlor.

"Felicity!" Annabelle exclaimed. "You look more unkempt than usual. I wouldn't be surprised if you had been climbing trees all morning!"

Annabelle always had something mean to say about Felicity. But Felicity was in too bright a mood to be bothered by snobby Annabelle Bananabelle. Besides, Annabelle sneezed and couldn't say anything else disagreeable.

"Bless you, my dear," Miss Manderly said as she entered the parlor.

Felicity curtsied. "Good day, Miss Manderly. These are for you," she said, presenting the flowers to the gentlewoman. "They are the first blossoms from our garden."

Miss Manderly smiled. "How thoughtful of you, Felicity," she said.

Elizabeth smiled, too. "Flowers! How lovely."

Annabelle did not smile. She sneezed. Then she sneezed again. Miss Manderly rang for her maidservant, who took the flowers away. "I fear the flowers may not be as delightful for Annabelle," she said. "I shall enjoy them in another part of the house."

Annabelle blew her nose, and then she flashed a satisfied smirk at Felicity. *You see*, Annabelle's look said. *Even your flowers are not quite proper.*

"Young ladies," Miss Manderly said, "we will continue our dancing lesson from yesterday. Let us take the same partners. Elizabeth, you and I will dance together. Annabelle, you will be Felicity's partner."

Felicity sighed. She was not a good dancer, no matter whom she danced with, but dancing with Annabelle made Felicity even more nervous. Elizabeth gave her friend a sympathetic look as they took their places.

Felicity did her best to follow Miss Manderly's instructions, but her dance looked quite different from everyone else's. She turned too soon and sank down too late. She hopped when no one else hopped. Annabelle was no help. She sighed impatiently when Felicity turned the wrong way, and she rolled her eyes when Felicity stepped forward instead of back.

Felicity was trying very hard not to step on Annabelle's foot again. She had done so the day before and had gotten quite a scolding from Annabelle. Fortunately, Felicity managed to keep away from Annabelle's feet.

Unfortunately, Felicity swung her leg at the wrong moment and kicked Annabelle in the knee with a solid thunk!

"My knee! Oh, my knee!" moaned Annabelle.

"I'm terribly sorry," Felicity apologized. Her face was red with embarrassment.

"You clumsy girl!" Annabelle screeched, rubbing her knee. "Another day of dancing with you and I shall be bruised all over."

"Annabelle!" said Miss Manderly firmly.

"That will do. Felicity has apologized. I know she is doing her best to be careful."

Felicity felt as though her bright mood had been carried out of the room with her flowers. When the dancing lesson was over, Elizabeth put her hand reassuringly on Felicity's shoulder. "Come to my house tomorrow," she whispered so that Annabelle couldn't hear. "I'll help you practice!"

The next day, as Felicity was preparing to leave for Elizabeth's house, her sister, Nan, begged to join her.

"Oh, please, Lissie. May I come along?" Nan asked eagerly. She loved dancing as much as Felicity hated it. Nan wanted very much to learn the steps Miss Manderly was teaching her older sister.

"I will teach you the dance, but not today," Felicity answered as she hurried to put on her hat. "It won't do for me to show you until I have learned it properly." Before Nan could say another word, Felicity was out the door.

It was another bright and breezy afternoon,

so Felicity and Elizabeth decided
to practice in the garden. The
apple trees were heavy with pink
blossoms, and the air was filled with
their delicious scent. Violets, pansies,
and sweet William grew in neat borders along
the path, and lilacs bloomed on the bushes.

Felicity took a deep breath of the fragrant
air. "I wish we were here to pick flowers rather
than practice dance steps," she sighed.

"That will be our reward when we have
finished," said Elizabeth. "Now, let's begin,"
she added, sounding very much like Miss
Manderly.

Elizabeth also danced very much like
Miss Manderly, for she had memorized each
movement exactly the way it had been taught.
Felicity tried to match her own hops, steps,
and turns to Elizabeth's, but her feet got just
as tangled out in the garden as they had in
Miss Manderly's parlor. But Elizabeth did not
give up. "Try again, Felicity," she encouraged.
Felicity grew red-faced and flustered, but she

kept trying. *At least Annabelle isn't here to point out my mistakes*, Felicity thought. But then Felicity heard a giggle.

Felicity stopped dancing and turned to Elizabeth. It wasn't like her friend to laugh at her! But Elizabeth wasn't laughing—she was counting out the steps. She stopped when she saw Felicity looking at her.

"Lissie, what's wrong?" Elizabeth asked.

Felicity was puzzled. "Did you hear someone laughing?"

"Here in the garden?" asked Elizabeth, looking about. "'Tis just the two of us, and I heard nothing. Come, let's try the step again."

Elizabeth started counting again in her soft voice, and Felicity tried to follow. "Step on one, sink down on two, step three—" She stopped suddenly. Elizabeth had heard it, too. Someone was in the garden, and someone was giggling. The girls looked under benches and behind bushes. Then Elizabeth pointed to a stirring in the flowering shrub.

"Annabelle!" said Elizabeth sternly. "I know

it's you. Come out of there!"

The branches of the bush rustled, and then Felicity and Elizabeth heard footsteps scurrying down the path on the other side of the tall hedge. They picked up their skirts and

ran through the arbor to the other side of the garden, but they were too late. The lawn was empty. Whoever had been giggling was gone.

Elizabeth was quite cross. "That Annabelle," she fumed. "She has no call to mistreat a guest in our home!"

"I wouldn't expect Annabelle to miss a chance to laugh at me," Felicity agreed. "But this is one time I'm quite certain Annabelle is not to blame."

Why was Felicity so sure Annabelle wasn't the one laughing? Turn to page 59 to find out.

It was salmon fishing time, and several Nez Perce villages had gathered near Celilo Falls. In the late afternoon, when the tasks of catching, cleaning, and smoking the salmon were done for the day, Kaya and her friends came together for games and tests of skill. Kaya's favorites were games played on horseback.

One afternoon Kaya and her friends Raven, Fox Tail, Two Hawks, and Yellow Moon decided to hold a horse race. When Kaya's older sister, Brown Deer, gave the signal to start, Kaya leaned forward and galloped Steps High as fast as she could. In a cloud of dust, the five horses crossed the finish line, each within a few seconds of the others.

"That was quite a race!" said Brown Deer, as she caught up with the riders at the finish line. "Your horses were so close the whole time, and with all the dust, from where I was standing I couldn't tell what order you came in."

"I didn't beat Kaya, but I outran Yellow

Moon," said Fox Tail, patting his horse.

"Steps High and I were right behind Two Hawks," said Kaya.

"Kaya came in just ahead of me," said Raven.

Can you figure out the order in which the riders finished the race? Check your answer on page 60.

Molly carefully cut the article from the front page of the newspaper. *Just wait until Dad sees this*, she thought. The article was all about the project the girls in Molly's class had done for the school's Lend-A-Hand contest. Molly remembered the rainy Saturday afternoon the ten of them had gathered at Alison Hargate's house to knit socks to help the war effort. None of the girls were very good knitters. Most of them had only knitted the top part of one sock. The little squares were about the size of a doll's blanket.That's when Molly had had the idea to turn all their small squares into one big blanket. Now the blanket was on its way to the hospital in England where Molly's father worked.

When Molly finished clipping the article from the paper, she began writing a letter to her dad. *I'll tell him who knit which squares*, she thought as she pulled a clean sheet of paper from her box of stationery. The trouble was, Molly was having a hard time remembering who had knit what. *I know*, Molly decided as

Knit One, Purl Who?

she pulled out a second piece of paper. *I'll write down what I remember. Then I'll figure out the rest.*

Here's what Molly wrote:

1. Alison did not knit the red squares.

2. Grace knit the orange squares.

3. Betty, Susan, Doris, and Shirley did not knit the pink squares.

4. Barbara's squares were the same color as the stars on an American flag.

5. Shirley's favorite color is blue, but she didn't knit those squares.

6. Linda, Alison, and Mary Lou did not knit the black squares.

7. Doris knit the tan squares.

8. Betty's squares were Shirley's favorite color.

9. Susan did not knit the green, black, or red squares.

10. Mary Lou and Alison both brought green yarn, but Mary Lou did not use it.

11. Linda knit the red squares.

Knit One, Purl Who?

Can you determine which color squares each girl knit? Fill in the chart below. To check your answers, turn to page 60.

	Blue	Tan	Green	Pink	Yellow	Brown	Orange	White	Black	Red
Alison					No					
Susan					No					
Linda					No					
Molly	No	No	No	No	Yes	No	No	No	No	No
Grace					No					
Mary Lou					No					
Betty					No					
Shirley					No					
Doris					No					
Barbara					No					

JEFFERSON DAILY NEWS

Molly McIntire and her teacher, Miss Charlotte Campbell, with winning project

Addy whistled as she set the table for breakfast. The dining room was the cheeriest place in the boarding house, and Addy loved to help Mrs. Golden get the morning meal ready. After Addy laid out the bowls, spoons, and glasses, she opened the drawer of the sideboard to fetch the napkins.

Each boarder's napkin was kept in a napkin ring with a number on it, so Addy could tell whose napkin was whose.

"Mr. Golden, Mrs. Golden, M'Dear, Momma, me, Miss Baxter, Poppa, Mrs. Sheridan, and Mr. Irving," Addy recited as she arranged the napkins in order from one to nine. Momma, Poppa, and Miss Baxter all had to be at work very early, so they wouldn't be having breakfast with the rest of the group. M'Dear wasn't feeling well this morning, so she was staying in her room. Addy put napkins three, four, six, and seven back into the drawer of the sideboard and set the others around the table.

The Spotless Stain

The smell of coffee filled the air, and Mrs. Golden carried a bowl of hot porridge in from the kitchen. "What a help you are, Addy," Mrs. Golden said. "Would you ring the kitchen bell?"

"Yes, ma'am," Addy agreed happily. She skipped into the kitchen, took the bell from the shelf, and shook it. The bright sound told the boarders that it was time to come to the dining room and eat.

Everyone was seated when Mr. Irving said, "Mrs. Golden, you must not have slept at all if you had time to wash the napkins since last night's supper." He placed his napkin on his knee and his napkin ring on the table.

Mrs. Golden looked puzzled. "Why, no," she said. "The napkins are going in today's wash."

"Then that's very strange," Mr. Irving answered. "I spilled some gravy on this napkin last night, and now there's not a sign of it anywhere." He turned the napkin over and over looking for the stain.

Everyone at the table looked perplexed. They pulled their own napkins out of the small metal rings and studied the white cloth. After a moment, Addy began to giggle. "The stain is still there, Mr. Irving," she said, standing up. "I can show you."

What did Addy show Mr. Irving? The answer is on page 60.

Molly loved Camp Gowonagin—the activities, the songs, and the sense of fun and cameraderie she felt with the other campers. So when Miss Butternut, the camp director, divided the girls into teams for the Color War, Molly couldn't wait to start planning strategy with her team, the Blue Army.

The next day, however, Molly discovered that the Blue Army captain, Dorinda Brassy, had already planned out the entire strategy on her own. Molly didn't quite know what to make of Dorinda. She was an older girl and had been to Camp Gowonagin many times before. Molly envied Dorinda's self-assurance, but there was something about her that made Molly uncomfortable.

As she sat in the boathouse with the rest of the Blue Army watching Dorinda announce the Color War strategy, Molly felt more and more uneasy. Dorinda seemed so confident, but her plan was—well, the plain truth was that the plan was too simple! If the Blue Army all paddled their canoes to the island, as Dorinda wanted, the Red Army would see them coming and be ready to capture them as soon as they landed.

Molly stood up and politely tried to explain the problem. "Won't they have scouts who will see us coming across the lake?" she asked.

"How do *you* think we should cross the lake?" Dorinda asked sharply. "Should we swim underwater?"

Molly felt a wave of shame. Everyone at camp knew she hated to swim underwater. Still, she tried to press her point, but Dorinda cut her off.

"If you are too chicken to do this, you can stay behind. Be a deserter," Dorinda taunted.

Shamed into silence, Molly sat down without another word.

"Now, to the canoes!" said Dorinda, and everyone filed out of the boathouse.

As she walked to the lake with Susan, her canoe partner, Molly tried hard to forget Dorinda and focus instead on helping her team

Red, Blue, and White

win. But it wasn't easy. Dorinda and her canoe partner were striding along shouting "Left, left, left-right-left," just as if they were marching in a real army. Molly couldn't help noticing scornfully how long and pale Dorinda's bare arms and legs looked. *She looks like a tall, gawky white stork*, Molly thought to herself.

As the girls settled into their canoes, Dorinda called to the Blue Team one more time. "It's a good thing I'm captain, because I've done lots of canoeing already this summer," Dorinda said. "In fact, I've been boating or swimming just about every day. With all my experience, we're guaranteed to win the Color War. All right, everyone start paddling—on the double!"

Susan looked at Molly and rolled her eyes. "Dorinda's kind of stuck-up, isn't she," she whispered.

Molly nodded. In fact, she now realized Dorinda was worse than stuck-up. She was a liar.

Why did Molly think this? Turn to page 60 to find out.

"Let's go!" Samantha said as she pulled a pair of ice skates from the pile on the front porch. "Last one on the ice is a frozen fish!"

Nellie, Ruth, Ida, and Helen shrieked with laughter as they raced after Samantha down the snowy path to Culpepper's Pond. Skates dangled from their arms, swinging and clanking as they ran. At the pond's edge, the girls flopped onto a bench and began the process of buckling ice skates on over their boots.

Suddenly Samantha stopped. "Wait a minute," she said. "These skates are brown. Mine are black!" She peered closely at the skates. "And these look quite new, while mine are worn and scuffed."

"Perhaps I've got yours, then," said Ruth, holding up a pair of skates. "These are black, like mine, but I see now they're very old and worn, while mine are new. Besides, these are much too small to fit my boots."

"My feet are even larger than yours," said Samantha. "If those skates are too small for *your* boots, they'd never fit mine."

Helen spoke up. "My mother just bought me brand new skates, and they're brown. Perhaps those are mine," she said, pointing to the skates Samantha was holding.

Samantha shook her head. "No, you've got small feet also, Helen, so these skates can't be yours if they fit me."

"Well, the ones I'm wearing certainly aren't mine—they're much too big!" Helen exclaimed. "Who owns a pair of new black skates fit for large boots?" She held them up.

"These skates aren't mine, either," Nellie said quietly as she unbuckled a pair of new brown skates with shiny blades. "They're quite small and they fit my boots, but my own skates are old and rusty. Besides, mine are black."

"I own a pair of new brown skates, but they'd be much too big for your little boots," said Ida, looking first at Nellie's small feet and then at her own. "The skates I'm wearing fit me all right, but they're black and quite scuffed, so I know they're not mine."

"Oh dear," said Nellie. "It seems that in our haste to get out on the ice, we each grabbed the wrong pair of skates!"

"It's all your fault, Samantha," said Ruth with a mischievous twinkle. "None of us wanted to be a frozen fish!"

Can you help the girls figure out which skates are whose? Read the story again carefully. As you read, note the descriptions of the skates worn by and owned by each girl in the tables on page 58. (The first table has been done for you.) Then compare the tables to figure out whose skates each girl was wearing! Check your answers on page 61.

Five Pairs of Skates Worksheet

SAMANTHA	Skates she was wearing:	Skates she owns:
brown or black?	brown	black
large or small?	large	large
old or new?	new	old

Samantha was wearing skates that belonged to ....

RUTH	Skates she was wearing:	Skates she owns:
brown or black?		
large or small?		
old or new?		

Ruth was wearing skates that belonged to ....

HELEN	Skates she was wearing:	Skates she owns:
brown or black?		
large or small?		
old or new?		

Helen was wearing skates that belonged to ....

NELLIE	Skates she was wearing:	Skates she owns:
brown or black?		
large or small?		
old or new?		

Nellie was wearing skates that belonged to ....

IDA	Skates she was wearing:	Skates she owns:
brown or black?		
large or small?		
old or new?		

Ida was wearing skates that belonged to ....

Answers

When Amos returned to the classroom, the bucket was filled to the top with water. If he had run all the way back from the stream, some of the water would have spilled out and the bucket wouldn't be nearly as full.

An Amusing Drive

When Bridget and Jenny told Aunt Cornelia all about their ride and the funny things Uncle Gard had said, Cornelia misheard. She thought they said, "If I hit a rock while I'm driving, I won't **brake**—I'll bounce!" That made her think Gard wasn't using his brakes if he hit something. The words *break* and *brake* sound just alike!

M, the last letter in the bottom row of a typewriter (or computer) keyboard!

Treasure in the Corn

Clara found the worm! Josefina was two, Clara was five, Francisca was eight, and Ana was twelve.

Riddle Me This

A piano is like a door because they both have keys. A comb has teeth but doesn't bite.

Giggles in the Garden

The flowers Felicity brought to Miss Manderly's house made Annabelle sneeze. Had Annabelle been in the garden watching Felicity and Elizabeth practice, the girls would have heard her sneezing—not giggling. It was Nan who had been watching Felicity and Elizabeth, and Nan who had been laughing.

59

Red, Blue, and White

If Dorinda had been boating or swimming just about every day that summer, as she claimed, she would not have been pale and white-skinned!

Kaya's Horse Race

The riders' order was Two Hawks, Kaya, Raven, Fox Tail, Yellow Moon.

The Spotless Stain

Addy went to the sideboard, opened the drawer, and pulled out the napkin with the gravy stain. Mr. Irving's napkin was in ring number nine. Addy had given him ring number six, which was Miss Baxter's napkin. When Addy had lined up the napkins that morning, she had read numbers six and nine upside down and had given Mr. Irving the wrong napkin.

The Ice Cream Culprit

Eddie appeared to have no idea why the girls were angry—but then he said, "I didn't put any salt in your ice cream." If he didn't know why the girls were angry, he wouldn't have known that there was salt in the ice cream—unless he had put it there himself!

What's In a Name

Frankie Jones, Georgia Frank, and Joanie St. George

Knit One, Purl Who?

Alison: green	Molly: yellow	Betty: blue
Susan: brown	Grace: orange	Shirley: black
Linda: red	Mary Lou: pink	Doris: tan
		Barbara: white

Five Pairs of Skates

SAMANTHA	Skates she was wearing:	Skates she owns:
brown or black?	brown	black
large or small?	large	large
old or new?	new	old

Samantha was wearing skates that belonged to Ida.

RUTH	Skates she was wearing:	Skates she owns:
brown or black?	black	black
large or small?	small	large
old or new?	old	new

Ruth was wearing skates that belonged to Nellie.

HELEN	Skates she was wearing:	Skates she owns:
brown or black?	black	brown
large or small?	large	small
old or new?	new	new

Helen was wearing skates that belonged to Ruth.

NELLIE	Skates she was wearing:	Skates she owns:
brown or black?	brown	black
large or small?	small	small
old or new?	new	old

Nellie was wearing skates that belonged to Helen.

IDA	Skates she was wearing:	Skates she owns:
brown or black?	black	brown
large or small?	large	large
old or new?	old	new

Ida was wearing skates that belonged to Samantha.